W9-BNS-781

BASKETBALL'S RECORD BREAKERS

BY SHANE FREDERICK

CAPSTONE PRESS
a capstone imprint

Sports Illustrated Kids Record Breakers is published in 2017
by Capstone Press, 1710 Roe Crest Drive, North Mankato, Minnesota 56003
www.mycapstone.com

Library of Congress Cataloging-in-Publication Data is available on the Library of Congress website.

ISBN 978-1-5157-3759-9 (library binding)
ISBN 978-1-5157-3763-6 (paperback)
ISBN 978-1-5157-3772-8 (eBook PDF)

Editorial Credits: Nick Healy, editor; Veronica Scott, designer; Eric Gohl, media researcher;
Gene Bentdahl, production specialist

Photo Credits
AP Photo: Paul Vathis, 5; Getty Images: Focus on Sport, 16, 18, 26, NBAE/Dick Raphael, 8, 27, Sports Illustrated/Greg Nelson, 12, Sports Illustrated/Rich Clarkson, 25 (right), Sports Illustrated/Walter Iooss Jr., 9, Sports Imagery/Herb Scharfman, 15; Newscom: EPA/John G. Mabanglo, 6, Icon SMI/Jeff Lewis, 4; Shutterstock: EKS, cover; Sports Illustrated: Al Tielemans, 23 (right), Andy Hayt, 10, David E. Klutho, 13, 28, Hy Peskin, 21, John Biever, 24, 25 (left), John D. Hanlon, 23 (left), John G. Zimmerman, 14, John W. McDonough, 11, 17 (right), 22, 29, Manny Millan, 7, 19, 20, Robert Beck, 17 (left)

Design Elements: Shutterstock

Printed in the United States of America.
112019   002869

TABLE OF CONTENTS

CHASING HISTORY

Kobe Bryant put on a show like few basketball fans had ever seen. Bryant's Lakers were playing in front of a home crowd at the glitzy Staples Center in Los Angeles, California, in January 2006. The Toronto Raptors simply couldn't stop Bryant. He made shot after shot after shot and led the Lakers to victory.

Bryant drained 28 baskets on 46 shots, including seven 3-pointers. He also made 18 of 20 free throws. When the final buzzer sounded, Bryant had 81 points. No player has come close to that number since.

Still, Bryant's staggering total wasn't a National Basketball Association (NBA) record. He couldn't quite match what the great Wilt Chamberlain had done 46 years earlier, although he came as close as anyone ever had.

Kobe Bryant

Chamberlain shocked the basketball world by scoring 100 points in a single game in March 1962. "The Big Dipper" made 36 of 63 field goals and 28 of 32 free throws. He led the Philadelphia Warriors to a win over the New York Knicks while posting the first and only triple-figure scoring performance in NBA history.

Wilt Chamberlain

RECORD BREAKERS

CHAMBERLAIN'S RECORD HAS LASTED FOR MANY YEARS, BUT IN THE NBA A RECORD CAN FALL ON ANY GIVEN NIGHT.

In 2015–16, the Golden State Warriors were the defending NBA champions, and they started the season by winning their first 24 games. During that run, people began to wonder if the "Splash Brothers"—long-range shooters Stephen Curry and Klay Thompson—had a chance to lead their team to 73 wins. That total would break what many fans thought was an unbreakable record: 72 victories by Michael Jordan and the Chicago Bulls in 1995–96.

Warriors fans urged the team toward a record-breaking win.

Late in the season, the Warriors were 69-8. They needed four wins in their final five games to break the record. They suffered a major setback, however, by losing an overtime game at home to the lowly Minnesota Timberwolves. (The T-wolves won just 29 games that season.)

The Warriors had four games left, and two of them were against the Western Conference's next best team, the San Antonio Spurs. It appeared Golden State might fall short of the record. But with Curry leading the way, Golden State pulled off the fantastic feat. Curry scored a total of 127 points in the final four games. That sum included 37 at San Antonio for win 72 and 46 at home against the Memphis Grizzlies for the record-breaker.

RECORD BUT NO CROWN

GOLDEN STATE'S 73-WIN SEASON WAS TARNISHED A BIT IN THE POSTSEASON. THE WARRIORS LOST TO THE CLEVELAND CAVALIERS IN THE NBA FINALS.

THE BULLS' RUN

When the Chicago Bulls won 72 games in 1995–96, they broke the Los Angeles Lakers' mark of 69 wins in 1971–72. The Bulls also won their fourth championship that year.

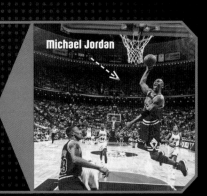
Michael Jordan

MOST WINS IN A SEASON

1. Golden State Warriors, 2015–16	73
2. Chicago Bulls, 1995–96	72
3. Los Angeles Lakers, 1971–72	69
3. Chicago Bulls, 1996–97	69
5. Philadelphia 76ers, 1966–67	68
5. Boston Celtics, 1972–73	68

JORDAN RULES

When the final buzzer sounded after the second overtime, the scoreboard showed the Boston Celtics had defeated the Chicago Bulls. The playoff game had pitted the aging Celtics against the upstart Bulls. While his team had been defeated, Michael Jordan won the moment.

Jordan scored 63 points in Boston Garden on that April day in 1986. His total broke a 24-year-old playoff record held by the Lakers' Elgin Baylor. Thirty years later, Jordan's 63 remains the NBA record for points in a playoff game.

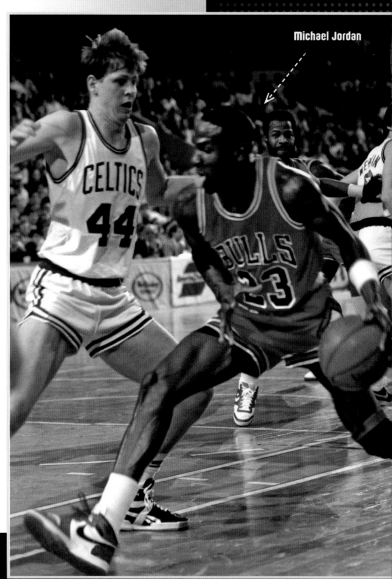

Michael Jordan

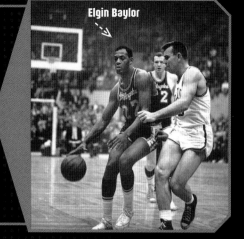
Elgin Baylor

FINALS RECORD

Elgin Baylor of the Los Angeles Lakers scored 61 points in a 126-121 victory over the Boston Celtics on April 14, 1962. Although Jordan holds the postseason record for points in a game, Baylor's feat remains the high mark for the NBA Finals.

Jordan was in his third NBA season, still five years away from winning his first of six NBA championships. But the superstar fans came to know was born in that game. He made 22 of 41 shots from the field and 19 of 21 from the free throw line. Those free throws included two in the final seconds of regulation—his 53rd and 54th points—to force the first overtime.

Even though the Celtics won the game and would go on to win the series, they were impressed with the young player. "I think he's God disguised as Michael Jordan," the legendary Larry Bird said afterward.

MOST POINTS IN A PLAYOFF GAME

1. **Michael Jordan, Bulls** (April 20, 1986)	63
2. **Elgin Baylor, Lakers** (April 14, 1962)	61
3. **Wilt Chamberlain, Warriors** (March 22, 1962)	56
3. **Michael Jordan, Bulls** (April 29, 1992)	56
3. **Charles Barkley, Suns** (May 4, 1994)	56

SKY'S THE LIMIT

Kareem Abdul-Jabbar perfected and made famous one of basketball's deadliest shots: the sky hook. The 7-foot-2 center turned his body sideways to the basket, raised the ball high above his head, and flicked the ball into the hoop. Opponents found the shot nearly impossible to block. Abdul-Jabbar used it to score thousands of points during his career.

Kareem Abdul-Jabbar

It was only appropriate that he turned to the sky hook to break the NBA's career scoring record in 1984. Facing the Utah Jazz, the Los Angeles Lakers star needed 22 points to break the record held by Wilt Chamberlain. In the fourth quarter, Abdul-Jabbar launched a sky hook high over the reach of shot-blocking center Mark Eaton. The shot dropped into the basket—and the record book.

Abdul-Jabbar accomplished the feat in his 15th NBA season. Chamberlain played 14 seasons. Abdul-Jabbar went on to play five more seasons and moved the record far beyond Chamberlain's mark. Abdul-Jabbar retired with 38,387 points.

CHASING KAREEM

Karl Malone of the Jazz came closer than anyone else to Abdul-Jabbar's record. Malone finished his career ranked second all-time with 36,928 points. Will anyone catch Abdul-Jabbar? Thirteen seasons into his career, LeBron James ranked 13th all-time with 26,833 points. He was 31 years old at that point. Abdul-Jabbar played until he was 42.

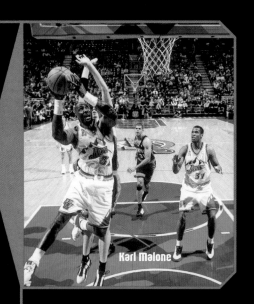

Karl Malone

CAREER POINTS

1. **Kareem Abdul-Jabbar** (Bucks, Lakers)	**38,387**
2. **Karl Malone** (Jazz, Lakers)	**36,928**
3. **Kobe Bryant** (Lakers)	**33,643**
4. **Michael Jordan** (Bulls, Wizards)	**32,292**
5. **Wilt Chamberlain** (Warriors, 76ers, Lakers)	**31,419**

TRIPLE THREAT

Stephen Curry took the ball off a screen, dribbled once between his legs and once behind his back, and then let the ball fly. As usual for the Golden State Warriors' sharpshooting point guard, the shot swished through the hoop. It was Curry's 11th three-pointer of the game and his 287th of the season, which broke his own NBA record from the year before.

Stephen Curry

The record-setting performance wasn't a big surprise. It was the third time Curry had set a new mark for three-pointers in a season. In 2012–13 he passed long-range specialist Ray Allen's 269 triples to set a new single-season record. Then Curry broke his own record two seasons later. What was special this time was that the 2016 game took place in late February. Almost two months remained in the regular season!

THE NBA ADDED THE THREE-POINT LINE IN THE 1979–80 SEASON. BRIAN TAYLOR OF THE SAN DIEGO CLIPPERS LED THE LEAGUE WITH 90 TRIPLES THAT SEASON.

Curry finished the game versus the Thunder with 46 points, including 12 three-pointers. He missed just four shots from beyond the arc. His final shot was a 35-footer to win the game in the final moments of overtime. By the end of the season, Curry had sunk 402 three-point shots, which was 116 more than his old record. He was named the league's most valuable player (MVP) for the season.

SHOOTER'S DOZEN

When Steph Curry made 12 three-pointers against the Thunder, he also tied the NBA record for the most triples in a game. Two other players in NBA history also had made that many—Los Angeles Lakers superstar Kobe Bryant in 2003 and journeyman Donyell Marshall, who downed a dozen in 2005 for the Toronto Raptors.

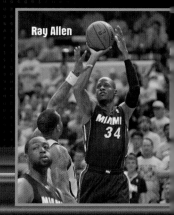

Ray Allen

CAREER 3-POINTERS

1. Ray Allen (Bucks, SuperSonics, Celtics, Heat)	**2,973**
2. Reggie Miller (Pacers)	**2,560**
3. Jason Terry (Hawks, Mavericks, Celtics, Nets, Rockets)	**2,169**
4. Paul Pierce (Celtics, Nets, Wizards, Clippers)	**2,128**
5. Jason Kidd (Mavericks, Suns, Nets, Knicks)	**1,988**

CRASHING THE BOARDS

Boston Celtics center Bill Russell pulled down 51 rebounds against the Syracuse Nationals on February 5, 1960. That total broke his own NBA record for rebounds in one game. Two seasons earlier, the 6-foot-10 Russell hauled in 49 rebounds in a game.

If there was any player capable of surpassing those amazing records, it was Wilt Chamberlain. "Wilt the Stilt," another powerful giant, was one of Russell's fiercest rivals.

Nine months after Russell's 51-rebound performance, he and his Celtics traveled to Philadelphia to face the 7-foot-1 Chamberlain and the Warriors. The game pitted the NBA's two best rebounders against each other. But that night Chamberlain dominated the glass. He surpassed Russell's record and finished the game with 55 rebounds.

Wilt Chamberlain

Chamberlain's record has not been touched. Since 2000, the most rebounds any player has had in a single game is 31. Kevin Love racked up that number while playing for the Minnesota Timberwolves in 2010.

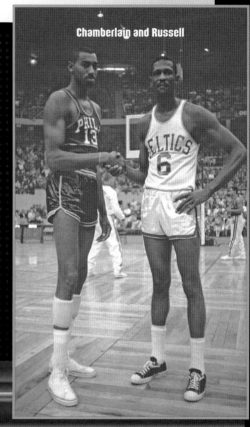

Chamberlain and Russell

GETTING OFFENSIVE

The NBA began keeping track of offensive rebounds in addition to total boards in 1973. Center Moses Malone proved among the best when it came to helping his team keep the ball after missed shots. In 1982 Malone set the league record for the most offensive rebounds in one game, pulling down 21.

CAREER REBOUNDS

1. **Wilt Chamberlain** (Warriors, 76ers, Lakers)	**23,924**
2. **Bill Russell** (Celtics)	**21,620**
3. **Kareem Abdul-Jabbar** (Bucks, Lakers)	**17,440**
4. **Elvin Hayes** (Rockets, Bullets)	**16,279**
5. **Moses Malone** (Braves, Rockets, 76ers, Bullets, Hawks, Bucks, Spurs)	**16,212**

PASSING FANCY

The game between the Orlando Magic and the high-scoring Denver Nuggets was a fast-paced, back-and-forth affair. For Magic point guard Scott Skiles, it was the perfect night for a record-setting performance.

Skiles dealt the nifty passes, and his teammates drained their shots. That meant Skiles was racking up assists. Early in the fourth quarter, he recorded his 20th assist, a rare feat for even the best point guards.

Then, with less than 30 seconds left in the game, Skiles passed the ball to teammate Jerry "Ice" Reynolds, who stopped and popped a jump shot. The basket was good, and Skiles had his 30th assist of the game. That gave him one more than the previous NBA record, set by the New Jersey Nets' Kevin Porter in 1978.

Scott Skiles

Skiles scored 22 points in the 155-116 victory, leading some to wonder if he could have had even more assists. Still, Skiles' record has stood ever since the December 30, 1990, win over the Nuggets.

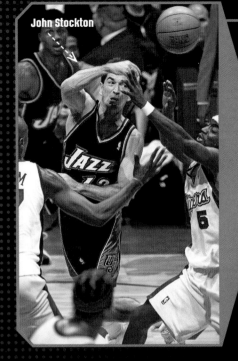

John Stockton

DYNAMIC DUO

Utah Jazz teammates John Stockton and Karl Malone formed one of the great passer-scorer combinations in NBA history. The two played together for 18 seasons. Stockton became the NBA's all-time leader in assists. Most of those assists were feeds to Malone, who ranks second on the career scoring list.

JOHN STOCKTON ALSO OWNS THE NBA RECORD FOR CAREER STEALS WITH 3,265.

Jason Kidd

CAREER ASSISTS

1. **John Stockton** (Jazz)	**15,806**
2. **Jason Kidd** (Mavericks, Suns, Nets, Knicks)	**12,091**
3. **Steve Nash** (Suns, Mavericks, Lakers)	**10,335**
4. **Mark Jackson** (Knicks, Clippers, Pacers, Nuggets, Raptors, Jazz, Rockets)	**10,334**
5. **Magic Johnson** (Lakers)	**10,141**

SIR SWAT

In the two years between having Wilt Chamberlain and Kareem Abdul-Jabbar on their roster, the Los Angeles Lakers employed Elmore Smith as their center. He didn't go on to the Hall of Fame as the other two did. Still, Smith earned a spot in the history books.

Elmore Smith

SHOT BLOCKERS

Center Hakeem Olajuwon, who spent all but one of his 18 seasons with the Houston Rockets, owns the career record for blocked shots with 3,830. Center Mark Eaton of the Utah Jazz set the single-season record with 456 rejections in 1984–85.

The 7-footer blocked 17 shots in a victory over the visiting Portland Trail Blazers on October 28, 1973. That season was the first year that blocked shots were kept as an official NBA statistic. There's no telling if Chamberlain, Celtics great Bill Russell, or another legend of earlier times had swatted away more shots in a single game. However, Smith's record has stood ever since.

The closest anyone has come to "The Rejector," as Smith was known during his career, was 15 blocks. Washington Bullets giant Manute Bol reached that number twice. Shaquille O'Neal did it once during his early years as a member of the Magic.

GREAT HEIGHTS

Manute Bol was one of the two tallest men ever to play in the NBA. He and Gheorghe Muresan each stood 7-foot-7. Bol is the only player in NBA history with more blocked shots (2,086) than points (1,599).

Manute Bol

The Los Angeles Lakers were celebrating their 2009 NBA championship. Their coach, Phil Jackson, put on a gold cap with a purple X—the Roman numeral 10—on its front. Ten was the number of titles Jackson had won as a head coach. That moved him past a record held for 43 years by the Celtics' Red Auerbach.

In Boston, Auerbach won nine titles in 10 years, including eight in a row between 1959 and 1966. He coached legendary players such as Bill Russell, John Havlicek, Bob Cousy, and Sam Jones.

Phil Jackson (right) with superstars Scottie Pippen (33) and Michael Jordan (23)

Jackson also coached legendary players while winning 11 titles in 20 years. With the Bulls, he coached Michael Jordan and Scottie Pippen to six crowns in the 1990s. When he took over as coach in Los Angeles, Jackson had Kobe Bryant and Shaquille O'Neal for three championships in a row between 2000 and 2002. O'Neal was gone for Jackson's record-breaker. Bryant was still there, however, and the Lakers had another top center in Pau Gasol.

GREEN IS GOOD

The Celtics have won more NBA titles than any other franchise with 17. No player owns more championship rings than Bill Russell, who was part of 11 of those Boston wins. The Lakers have won 16 championships. That total includes 11 in Los Angeles and five during the team's early years in Minneapolis.

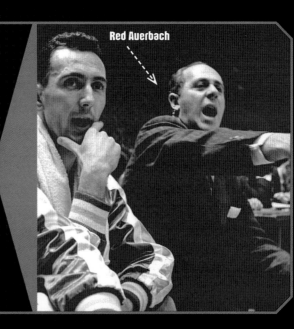
Red Auerbach

STILL WAITING

The Cleveland Cavaliers won the 2016 title, the first trophy in franchise history. After that the NBA was left with 10 teams without a championship trophy. Those 10 have never won a championship in either the NBA or the American Basketball Association (ABA). They are the Charlotte Hornets, Denver Nuggets, Los Angeles Clippers, Memphis Grizzlies, Minnesota Timberwolves, New Orleans Pelicans, Orlando Magic, Phoenix Suns, Toronto Raptors, and Utah Jazz.

The Miami Heat made an incredible run for nearly two months during the 2012–13 season. Led by stars LeBron James, Dwyane Wade, Chris Bosh, and Ray Allen, the Heat rattled off 27 wins in a row. The Heat couldn't quite match the NBA's longest streak, though.

That record still belongs to the 1971–72 Los Angeles Lakers, who won 33 consecutive games. Jerry West, Gail Goodrich, Wilt Chamberlain, and their teammates defeated their opponents by an average of 17 points a game. The winning streak stretched more than 65 days. The Lakers were finally halted by the Milwaukee Bucks. The Bucks had held the previous record of 20 wins in a row. They were led by a player who would one day join the Lakers, the great Kareem Abdul-Jabbar.

LeBron James with the 2012-13 Heat.

Jerry West

The Golden State Warriors came as close to the Lakers' run as any team. They won 28 games in a row. Their streak started with four victories to close out the 2014–15 regular season and continued with 24 wins to start 2015–16.

ROUGH ROAD

The longest losing streak in NBA history belongs to the Philadelphia 76ers, who dropped 28 games in a row between two seasons in 2015. The longest losing streak in the same season is 26 games. The 2010–11 Cleveland Cavaliers endured that slump.

THE 76ERS LOST A RECORD 73 GAMES DURING THE 1972–73 SEASON. IN 2015–16 THEY LOST 72 GAMES.

DOUBLE TROUBLE

Reaching double-digits in any statistical category usually means a good night for a professional basketball player. Doing it in multiple categories is often a sign of a special performance. Players such as Wilt Chamberlain and Bill Russell racked up many double-doubles in their time as they dominated scoring and rebounding. During one long stretch, Chamberlain had 227 in a row.

After the NBA and ABA merged in 1976, such streaks became rare. In 1978–79 the Rockets' Moses Malone reeled off 51 games in a row with at least 10 points and 10 rebounds. That was the longest streak until 2011, when the Timberwolves' Kevin Love challenged and surpassed it.

Kevin Love

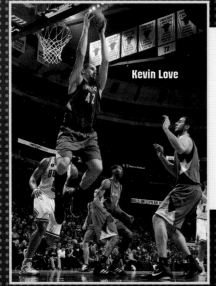
Kevin Love

Love had made his name as a smart rebounder who read the angles of missed shots. His 52nd double-double in a row came when he scored 16 points and pulled down 21 boards against the Indiana Pacers. He reached 53 before the streak ended with a six-point, 12-rebound game.

Oscar Robertson

TRIPLE THREAT

Oscar Robertson of the Cincinnati Royals had an amazing season in 1961–62. He averaged a triple-double, scoring 30.8 points, grabbing 12.5 rebounds, and dishing out 11.4 assists per game. "The Big O" holds the record of most triple-doubles in a career (181) and a season (41).

QUADRUPLE DOUBLES

David Robinson (Spurs), 1994	34 points, 10 rebounds, 10 assists, 10 blocks
Hakeem Olajuwon (Rockets), 1990	18 points, 16 rebounds, 10 assists, 11 blocks
Hakeem Olajuwon (Rockets), 1990	29 points, 18 rebounds, 10 assists, 11 blocks
Alvin Robertson (Spurs), 1986	20 points, 11 rebounds, 10 assists, 10 steals
Nate Thurmond (Bulls), 1974	22 points, 14 rebounds, 13 assists, 12 blocks

RUN AND GUN

Kiki Vandeweghe

For basketball fans who liked offense but didn't care much for defense, the 1981–82 Denver Nuggets were a dream team. That season the high-flying Nuggets raced up and down the court. They scored an NBA-record 126.5 points per game. They also allowed an average of 126 points per game. Alex English, Dan Issel, and Kiki Vandeweghe starred for the team. Each of them averaged more than 20 points a game, and the Nuggets never finished with fewer than 100 points in a game that season.

The NBA introduced the 24-second shot clock in 1954 to increase scoring. Before that the game was played slowly, with dull, plodding offenses. Teams holding leads often stalled, and defenses could only foul to try to get the ball back. The shot clock dramatically picked up the pace. It forced teams to take shots or lose possession of the ball.

Two seasons later, coach Doug Moe's Nuggets played in the highest-scoring game in NBA history. They fell 186-184 to the Detroit Pistons in triple overtime on December 13, 1983. The 370 combined points broke the record of 337 total points in a game. That number had come in a triple-overtime game between the Milwaukee Bucks and San Antonio Spurs in 1982.

Doug Moe

The Nuggets-Pistons game was also remarkable because two players from each team scored more than 40 points. They were Isiah Thomas (47) and John Long (41) of the Pistons and Vandeweghe (51) and English (47) of the Nuggets.

THE LOWEST-SCORING GAME IN NBA HISTORY OCCURRED ON NOVEMBER 22, 1950—FOUR YEARS BEFORE THE SHOT CLOCK WAS INTRODUCED. THE FORT WAYNE PISTONS DEFEATED THE MINNEAPOLIS LAKERS 19-18.

THE FUTURE

LeBron James became the youngest player in league history to score 5,000 points in the playoffs. He reached the mark while leading the Cavaliers to their first NBA championship. By the end of the 2016 Finals, James had 5,572 postseason points, which ranked fourth all-time. James was just 415 points behind record-holder Michael Jordan.

James entered the NBA straight out of high school at the age of 19. Through 2016, he had led his teams—the Cavaliers and the Heat—to the playoffs in 11 of his 13 seasons. Those teams advanced far too. The last six of them made it to the Finals, and three of them took home championships. Given his relative youth, James seems likely to break Jordan's playoff record.

LeBron James